DISQUIET THE HIDDEN DEPTHS OF MEN

SAM JUDGE

Introduction
Kevin Braddock

It's a contemporary cliché that men don't talk about their feelings. This cliché also illuminates another set of clichés upon which that one rests, including the idea men don't have feelings in any case (or indeed only the basest ones); that non-men naturally and automatically talk about their feelings; and finally that when men do talk, they only ever talk in objective terms—at best in a series of grunts, jokes, and critiques, expressing feeling through proxies: Saturday's match, a certain car or machine, about "birds" or the stressors impinging (bosses, cash flow, politicians, the daily hassle of sorting shit out).

It's true that it takes some effort to interpret what men are saying when they do speak about what Carl Rogers termed "the private perceptual world", which everyone, regardless of gender, possesses. And it's rarely easy for men to address, express, and make sense of this inner realm. This may in part be because they are rarely asked about it or offered a space in which to speak, along with the permission to do so. What's also true is that when men do finally open up, a surprising eloquence and articulacy often results. Confessions and admissions can be nuanced and moving, admitting the complexity of all feelings and their disorientating interplay with thoughts.

It shouldn't really be a surprise: centuries—millennia, in fact—of art, poetry, literature, music, philosophy, design, horticulture, and craft made by men from Bronzino to Ai Weiwei, or Chaucer to Houellebecq, contradict yet another cliché, the one suggesting men are merely left-brained, coldly analytical creatures, alienated from the realm of sensation, and never making things for the sake of their aesthetic beauty alone.

Perhaps this best sums up the feeling that animates *Disquiet: The Hidden Depths of Men* itself. It's an exploratory enterprise, an endeavour to know men by what they say when given the chance to unhide what's concealed. Men may not need to talk about their feelings and may, for many reasons, choose to keep them hidden. But we should admit that they deserve an opportunity to speak freely and openly. We needn't be too concerned with what keeps those things hidden and instead concentrate on the notion that men do feel feelings, and when they reveal them, something special often emerges.

Contents

In mid-2016 I shared my story of mental illness on the internet. It took me two years to feel ready to share it but only a few hours to write it. I didn't overthink sharing it online. Putting my experience into words felt like the natural way to make sense of it all—a deeply cathartic one too. Writer Will Oshiro de Groot took a similar approach, putting his feelings into words. In his case a letter to a friend, written whilst in the midst of a crisis. It is republished here as an important and timely letter to the world (page 36).

Shortly after I published my story, I began receiving messages from friends and colleagues. Each message was the same, they too had experienced something similar. My network is small; the number of people who have read the story is probably only in the hundreds. However, within this small circle was an overwhelming percentage of people who had experienced similar negative and distressing feelings. Despite rising media attention on the subject of mental illness, it was these personal messages that made the enormity of the problem truly apparent to me.

There are plenty of statistics on mental illness, but there are a few that help give context as to why I felt it necessary to create the pages you now hold in your hands. Suicide is the leading cause of death for men under 50 in the UK. Not only that, men are three times more likely to die by suicide than women.* An extraordinary imbalance, especially when women are almost twice as likely to be diagnosed with anxiety disorders.† So what gives?

* https://bit.ly/2eKq1V2 † https://bit.ly/1PTJXtG

An outdate
the archai
to fit, the a
"man up", j
to an inabi
their issue
today's me
stigmas ar
within thes
examples
never hear
their inner

model of masculinity,
nould men feel the need
oo damaging phrase
st a few things that lead
for men to talk about
Silence is what's killing
Change is happening,
being broken, and here
pages are perfect
that: some men you've
of, speaking honestly of
squiet.

—Sam Judge, Editor

THREE WEEKS TO GET USED TO THE TABLETS I WENT LOWER THAN EVER BEFORE

FRAZER LAWTON

Publicist, London

I first met Frazer when I moved into his flat share on Seven Sisters Road. On my first night in the flat we celebrated over a drink. It should have been an evening of small talk, filled with the typical questions people ask when getting to know each other. Instead, we shared our experiences of anxiety, medication, and therapy. It was an openness that is reflected in what follows. He gets it: only good can come of speaking honestly about these matters.

I had my first real episode of mental illness when I was 21. At the time, I had no idea that's what it was. I saw a doctor and she referred me to cognitive behavioural therapy. After waiting two months, I still hadn't heard anything back and I was getting desperate. It turned out the NHS had fucked up my referral. I felt completely hopeless; two months feels like forever when you're going through that. I ended up asking my parents for help. If they hadn't offered to pay for private therapy I'd have probably killed myself. Since then, I've continued with private therapy.

Finding a therapist is like dating someone. You've got to find someone who you get on with and who you feel is going to work for you. My first therapist was really sincere, which was great. She specialised in the queer community but what we spoke about wasn't really about me being gay; it was just about life. With my second therapist it felt like she was reading from a script. It didn't feel like she actually cared.

Working in the music industry, it's so easy to end up in an unhealthy pattern. I'll have to be at a gig that doesn't start until 9pm. I'll eat out, have a few drinks, probably head to the after-party, get wasted. It might sound like a good night, but I'm expected to be back in the office at 9am, on point. When I started out I viewed these as perks of the job. Ironically, the perks of the job have often become the reason why I've felt shit.

My anxiety got so bad that I couldn't go to work. I was at the door of my flat, ready to leave but I couldn't do it. It was like I was trying to force myself to get out. I was locked in my own mind and subsequently, my flat. I ended up having about three weeks off. Despite the way the industry is, my boss was really understanding. I told her everything. I felt, given the situation, it was important to be candid.

When I was younger I dealt with depression by going out and getting pissed. Now I'm getting a bit older, I've decided I need to deal with it another way. I can't just keep getting high. I try to eat well, I run, swim, do yoga. That worked for a while but more recently it got to the point where I felt like none of that was helping. That's when I decided to go on medication, because despite doing everything I possibly could, my anxieties had got to the point where they were stopping me from leaving the house.

“In sex education you’re taught that it’s a man and a woman. If you don’t fit that mould, how do you learn about relationships?”

It took three weeks to get used to the tablets. It was horrible. I went lower than I had ever been before. I knew I just had to ride it out. Then one day it cleared and I thought, *Thank god for that*. I felt like I was high, a little bit light-headed, or like I was floating.

Since then, taking Sertraline has made me feel so balanced out. Friends and parents have said that I’m back to the old Frazer. I don’t feel like I get the highs I used to get but I also don’t get the lows either. When I say highs I mean like how I’ve felt when I’ve been in love with someone. I’m hopeful though, that if I do meet someone, I’ll still get to feel that high. We’ll see.

I once signed up to do a sex course and it was weird as hell. I arrived at this place and there were five other guys standing there in a circle. I joined the group and we took turns to introduce ourselves. After that they got us on the floor doing mindfulness exercises. *So far so good*, I thought, but that’s when it got weird. Whilst we were lying there, eyes closed, they made us touch ourselves. I went on the course to learn to be comfortable with myself, not to learn how to be comfortable masturbating in a room full of strangers. If that wasn’t bad enough the instructor gave us homework. He told us, “Before you go to bed, look at yourself in the mirror naked and to write down what you see.” By that point I was thinking, *What the fuck is going on?* I had lost track of who I was. Needless to say, I didn’t go back the next day.

When I was growing up I struggled with not having someone to identify with. We live in a world where in films, TV programmes, and books it’s always a man and a woman. In sex education you’re taught that it’s a man and a woman. If you don’t fit that mould, how do you learn about relationships? Most people look to their parents or older siblings. But who’s that role model when you’re not like them? I don’t feel like I ever had that role model to look up to.

I've spent most of my adult life doing one-night stands. It was great to start with and I naïvely thought I could meet someone that way. Turns out, I wasn't ready. I'd get drunk or high to help me feel like casual sex was what I wanted but in the cold light of day, I'd wake up next to a guy and wished he would leave. I can see now that I wasn't comfortable with myself and so I didn't want a man in my bed. The underlying issue for me is that I need to learn how to be comfortable with who I am.

For years I've asked, "What's the reason I'm not comfortable with myself?" I've come to realise I'll probably never find that out. Instead, I think the key is to just be present. Don't look into the future; don't look into the past; just be present and happy with who you are at that moment in time. If my mind is somewhere else, I'm never going to be happy. I've tried to apply this and it's not always easy but I definitely feel more comfortable with myself than ever before.

Frazer

ALONE

COPE

MALE

REALITY

Owen Thomas
In conversation with Sam Judge

An elliptical stroll through four big questions on mental health and illness

Owen is a designer with whom I worked for a brief period. He is a talented and perceptive man, and able to talk in a nuanced way about some of the conflicts he deals with. What follows is an abridged version of a deeper discussion. It struck me how Owen made sense of things being a process rather than a destination, not unlike the walks he takes around London to find space in his mind.

How can we be alone with ourselves?

OT Today I wasn't having a great day so I took a long-ass walk. I walked all the way to Soho, saw a film and felt much better. I used to try and fight shitty days like this, but now I'll just wander for hours and take in the city. No intentions in mind, no end point, just wandering aimlessly. It's a good feeling and I need that sometimes. I see it as a way of centring myself. When I'm on a project I'm putting all of my energy into something else, which can feel great, but equally it's important I take time to collect myself and let everything settle back down before moving forward again.

SJ I can't remember the last time I was completely aimless.

OT Well you have a baby now, so I imagine it's near impossible.

SJ It feels like it at times. As much as I love my family, there are times when I can't help but crave being alone. I used to have lots of that alone time, and now I feel like I'm never alone.

OT That would be hard for me. I relish my alone time. I have waves where I need to be social and be surrounded by people but then other times where I need to withdraw and be on my own. If I go days on end where I don't have any time to be with myself then I'll start to get a bit anxious.

SJ After a busy week, Elle and I will be pottering about on a weekend and she'll ask out of the blue, "What's going on? You're not talking?" Then I'll realise I'm having something we now call a "quiet day". It's me needing to be alone yet still being in the presence of others.

OT I totally have those [laughs]. I just shut down sometimes.

I JUST SHUT DOWN SOMETIMES

How do we cope?

OT I was in a really crazy startup for a while. The CEO was an asshole and the hours were crazy. I was young and had no experience dealing with difficult people. Had I known more about depression and anxiety, I'd have dealt with it a different way. Instead, I just burned through the week and then let myself loose on booze. It was the only way I knew how to decompress. I see a lot of people deal with their problems that way. Go down to Liverpool Street on a Friday night and you can see it in action.

SJ Do you think they realise that it's a coping mechanism?

OT I don't think they do. I think there's a huge issue in Britain where people use alcohol to cope. It feels like people drink to make themselves stupid so they can let go of all this shit that built up over the week. It's incredibly unhealthy, but I'm as guilty of it as anyone.

SJ So how did you get through that?

OT I recognised that my drinking was a coping mechanism and started cognitive behavioural therapy. I needed to fix how I felt about my situation and how I dealt with my anxieties. There were some things that I took away from it, mostly around self-awareness and how much of an impact your own thought patterns can have on you.

For me, that was a big point. I needed that really hard period to help me realise that I had some problems I hadn't dealt with. Since then it has been a constant process of monitoring my anxiety. I'm now much more aware of how my thought patterns tend to get away from me when I start to feel anxious. It's about catching that early on before it gets too bad.

SJ It's interesting how you refer to monitoring your emotional state as a "constant process". Do you foresee an end point?

OT I see it as a process of maintenance rather than an end point. There's no end to it, like eating well or exercising; it just becomes another way in which you take care of yourself.

Equality: what's in it for men?

SJ Through my wife, I've become more aware of feminism and what that means to her. Reading as much as I can on the issue, and hearing about it from her side, I believe the real value I can add is by helping to change the perception of what it means to be a man. I strongly believe that if we can create a more flexible definition of masculinity, or better yet, help men become more comfortable with the idea of no definition of masculinity, then it will ultimately aid the goal of feminism.

OT It's a noble pursuit but to get there I think we need to create a deal between the sexes. Naturally, men ask of that deal, "What's in it for me?" Some men are bound to feel threatened by the prospect of equality. They thrive on dominance and being in a position of control. Getting towards equality will require men to step back.

SJ But telling anyone to take a step back doesn't sound very appealing. Especially when that person is a man who is used to being in a position of power. The argument for why equality is a good thing has to come from both sides, not only what women will gain, but also what benefits men can expect too.

OT You'd think it should come as a relief for men, surely?

SJ Exactly. Imagine the relief of realising that you don't need to fit a mould you've never felt able to fit.

Is mental illness a problem or a reality?

OT When we talk about "the fight" against mental illness it only serves to present it as a problem rather than a reality. Why do we always have to feel good? Why can't it be OK to just feel shit sometimes?

SJ I really hate this idea that we should strive to be happy all the time. So much of what we see online is pushing this ideal. We're made to feel like the highlights presented to us are how we should always be feeling. The fact that you've had a bad day shouldn't make you feel defeated; it should just be a part of what it is to be human.

OT Canada has a similar cultural issue. The baseline of what it is to be Canadian is this happy-go-lucky, at-ease persona. It has always grated on me. If anything, I'm the opposite of that. I'm highly strung, often anxious, deeply dissatisfied with how things are.

There's a naïveté in happiness. If you're completely and continually happy then you're ignorant to facts of life. There are other people in the world who aren't happy; there are things about life that aren't great, and where we're heading as a civilisation doesn't look good.

SJ As much as I believe that lauding happiness as the ultimate goal is a futile exercise, I struggle to think what other emotion would be appropriate? Is it contentment that we should strive for?

OT But what does that mean, "to be content"? I get a lot of my drive from being dissatisfied and having something I can work towards. Dissatisfaction isn't a bad thing, it just means that you want something to be better.

SJ So if discontent is needed to fuel creativity, what is the goal?

OT It's all suggesting that there's a right way to feel but I don't think there is one.

MAN

MICHAEL

ON

TOM

THE

WALKER

STREET

WAIT

Diptych 1
Dublin, Ireland
Havana, Cuba

Diptych 2
Hackney, London
Islington, London

Diptych 3
Havana, Cuba
Hackney, London

WATCHING MY BODY FROM A DISTANCE CARRYING OUT MY NORMAL ACTIVITIES

MICHAEL HATCHER

Programmer, Norwich

I worked with Mike for three years during my first design gig in London. He's incredibly funny and once you tune in to it, his humour is contagious. Break through that comic façade however, and what emerges is a sensitive and deeply introspective man. What resonated most for me was his unabating concern with his position in the world. He, like so many of us, often asks much more of himself than is reasonably healthy.

I've thought a lot about a world where we've cured depression, but I'm not sure that would be a good thing. So many amazing things in arts, media, and pop culture are driven by depression, anxiety, and people's insecurities. I think part of it is because they're compensating for the way they feel by driving themselves to do remarkable things. What if we were to eradicate depression and those feelings of insecurity in people? Would those people stop producing amazing things? Perhaps, but I think the important thing to recognise is that negative thoughts are a valuable part of creativity. Perhaps we should start thinking about depression and anxiety differently to channel it for our advantage.

The more I read into matters of the mind, the more worrying it becomes. I'd love to be able to read that kind of stuff and just be. Instead, I constantly feed that new information into how I feel about my own issues. I wonder whether all the people around me are blissfully unaware of all these mental health issues. Of course, I could never know for sure but I like to think that maybe, in their ignorance, they've got the right idea.

For the majority of my life I didn't have any plans of any sort, I just coasted. I hit 35 and I realised I had to start thinking about what the future holds. I decided to end things with my partner at the time, which brought about many emotional challenges. We began dating when we were both very young. It's easy when you're young. Nothing matters, you just sort of forge on. But I don't think we ever became anything other than two separate people. We never really got close emotionally and we never talked about anything big or important. As we got older, that division got deeper and became problematic.

Coming out of a long-term relationship had a big effect on me. I felt like I'd been through ten years of relative stability and then suddenly it all changed. It was like I was at square one, everything had reset. All of the things that had built up over a decade, all those memories, experiences, adventure, and material things as well, that was all behind me. Ending the relationship felt like the right thing to do, but despite believing that, it was still difficult to reconcile what felt like an enormous loss of time.

I think I've suffered from depression for longer than I've realised. I've lived with it for years but it wasn't until recently that it occurred to me that what I was feeling could be a clinical issue. I worry often. I worry about my position in the world and my position in life. I'm always asking myself, "Where should I be and why aren't I there?" I wouldn't say I've had suicidal thoughts but I've definitely questioned the purpose of my existence.

My biggest problem at the moment is general anxiety. It's hard to describe. It's a general unease and an adrenaline feeling all the time. I'm sometimes shaky, but not always, and I find it hard to relax, like properly relax, whatever that means. Feeling this way makes it really hard to focus on specific tasks for a long time, not great for a programmer.

I went through a big existential crisis that resulted in what I can only describe as an out-of-body experience. I had the flu at the time and suddenly started to feel detached from my body. At first, it was quite exciting and I thought I'd just go with it. For a week or so I was watching my body from a distance, carrying out my normal activities. It was like everything in the world and all of my experience was this one ball of concept. There was no difference between things, everything had become one in this weird way. My own identity seemed to completely disappear and I felt like I had no idea about my representation in the world. After a week of this, it dawned on me that what I was experiencing might be serious.

"Getting close to someone requires being vulnerable and revealing yourself. I don't know whether I've ever felt comfortable enough with anyone to do that."

I googled my symptoms and came across "borderline anxiety disorder". It seemed like a really good description of the way I was feeling. The more I read about it, the more it seemed to confirm my suspicions. However, I do wonder whether reading about it actually reinforced any of those behaviours.

Google can only go so far, so I decided to get professional help. At the time, all I really wanted to hear was confirmation, or otherwise, that I had a personality disorder. I couldn't really afford it so I only ended up having two sessions. Even still, it was a relief just to hear from a professional that he suspected I didn't have a personality disorder.

Talking to my parents was fucking useless. I had a great upbringing and we get on well but with my family nothing is ever very deep or meaningful, it's all very surface-level; banter and laughs. When I told them I was experiencing some issues, all I wanted was for them to be sympathetic and to listen. Instead, they just tried to brush it under the carpet.

I've gone through my entire life being this closed ball and never really opening up to anyone. Getting close to someone requires being vulnerable and revealing yourself. I definitely think I have trust issues. I believe that when you really trust someone you can tell them anything, but I don't think I've ever felt comfortable enough with anyone to do that.

FROM THE MARGINS

Words by Will Oshiro de Groot, founder of MEND, a platform that seeks to critically understand men, masculinity, and patriarchy in our culture.

February 2019

Last week on Wednesday, I phoned work to say I couldn't come in because, well...I felt like I physically couldn't be there. I had hit a wall emotionally, mentally, and physically and felt utterly exhausted. It took the help of my therapist for me to realise what was happening. That morning, she pointed out to me that I was trying to hold everything together, but that cracks were appearing. It was only then that I realised just how bad things had gotten. I was talking through strained eyes and a tense forehead. A voice that cracked, an exhausted spirit.

I left my session that morning and walked through Southwark crying. I was walking against the tide of the commuter path; a mass of breathing bodies at 9am. Cyclists, people on foot, people on buses. Everyone with that sole intent of getting to their final destination: to work—some place in the city, in some office, to sit for eight hours and stare at a screen. I walked past them all, acutely conscious that I was going in the opposite direction. The only place I needed to be was home. Today I didn't want to play.

On the bus home, I phoned work to say I needed to take time off. I called my colleague—someone I trust—in tears, telling him that I needed time off and time away. I'd simply had enough and felt that it was too much. It's difficult to describe that feeling of despair, of being trapped and being unable to see any way out. Pure exasperation. I have never known a tiredness like it; my face hurt, my head was constantly tense. It was like I'd been hit by a bus. I spent the next three days pretty much motionless on the sofa.[1]

1. I'm someone who's very comfortable doing nothing. On flights I never watch movies, instead I just sit, thinking and staring for hours. I was describing my experience of being mixed-race the other day to someone and explained that often the only place I ever really feel "at home" is on an airplane. Suspended, where nothing really matters, not really knowing where you are, what rules apply, or where physical and geographical boundaries begin and end. There's always a heaviness that lifts as the wheels of the aircraft leave the runway.

I've spent the previous month battling with various physical manifestations of what I now understand to be anxiety. Over time, these began increasing in their regularity.[2] It's funny how no one ever really teaches us how to listen to what our bodies are telling us, or to recognise that we might be shutting down. As I battled with physical sensations, I reflected on how I often feel pressured by a self-imposed expectation of fulfilling some kind of promise to myself, whatever that might be.

I woke up one Sunday that month with a real feeling of dread for the following Monday. I knew then that things were not OK. I needed to prepare for a meeting with a well-known multi-billion-dollar tech company. In my last encounter with them, I had given a presentation on what was going on in London in terms of lifestyle, beauty, brands, and culture. After presenting some work of young, black, British female entrepreneurs working in the hair-care space, one of the white male "creative directors" looked straight at me and said, "...and why do you think this is relevant for us?"

Anyone who knows this context in life will read the above and recognise the exact tone in which this question was asked. I had been asked to qualify and explain why black women and communities in London were of importance to their marketing and communications strategy. The difficulty of these situations is that, as people of colour, we are the only ones who can see (and crucially *feel*) these things in the room. Responsibility falls on us to explain the reality of lived experiences to people that aren't ready to hear—or don't deserve to hear—such stories and experiences. That feeling of frustration is my recognition of the fact that these people believe in the centring of their own experiences as the universal view.

We should no longer downplay the emotional labour of being the only person in the room. The person who is forced to engage in a defence of non-white people and culture, to validate and justify the existence of people of colour within a commercial setting against a wall of multi-million-dollar ignorance. These people—more often than not, white men—who can both figuratively and literally afford to be unaware, complacent, and mediocre. I reject the reasoning often used in response to these instances that emphasises the importance of *being in the room*, because being

2. An uncontrollable and persistent eye twitch. An occasional tingling sensation down my arm on my left side. An irregular and pronounced heart flutter, which felt like a caged and erratic pigeon trying to beat out of my chest. At times, I would feel dizzy or lose my balance, either sat at my desk or going down the escalator to get to the tube. A slight moment of hesitation between steps before balance would restore itself. I'd carry on like nothing happened. Afterwards I'd think, *that was new*, but quickly push it to the back of my mind, because thinking on it too long made it too real.

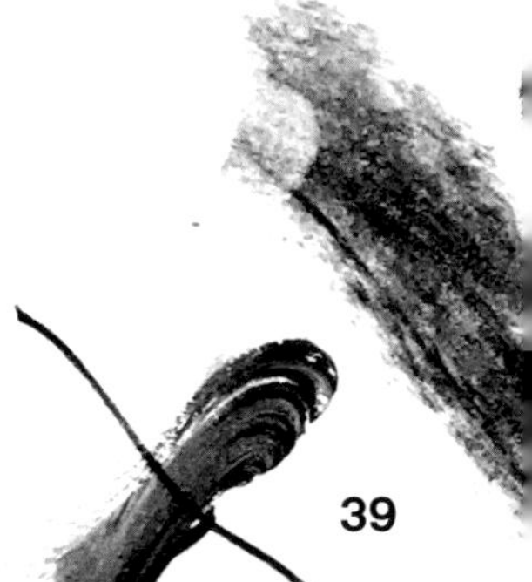

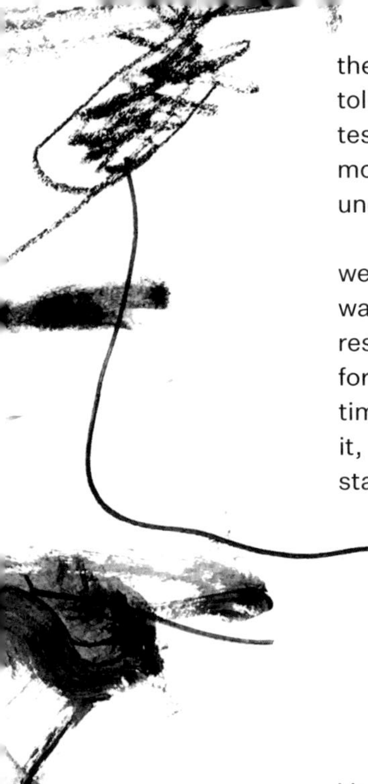

the only one in the room is exhausting and eventually will take its toll. These experiences and realisations are overwhelming. It is a testament to those of us who recognise this that we wake up every morning and continue to go to work in the face of this continued unchecked ignorance and flagrant stupidity.

Such was my month of January. I had deliberately kept my weekends low-key, aware of how tired I felt and of how much I wanted to rest at any given opportunity. But despite this illusion of rest, my body and my mind had been on a slow burn to this point for months before. Sometimes it was subtle and consistent, other times it was forceful, prominent, and painful. When I think about it, I realise now that these are symptoms and feelings that had started well before then.

Years before, in November 2017, I had suffered what I could only describe as a severe emotional breakdown. One evening, sat in the living room of a flat I was staying in at the time, I cried for what could have been two hours or more.[3] Unable to speak, jaw clenched, acutely aware of the disconnect between the thoughts in my head and my ability to form words. I sat head in hands, unable to prevent what felt like an outpouring of grief from my gut and behind my eyes. I had completely neglected myself and allowed others to take advantage of my better self. The expectations that had been placed on me had exceeded anything that had been fair or kind and when I failed to meet them, I had been left to question the very fundamentals of my nature and being. At worst, I had been made to believe that I was not a good person. It rocked and unnerved me to my very core.

3. In that moment, I can only describe what felt like a severing between my thoughts and my speech. It terrified me beyond anything that I had previously known or experienced. I had hit a wall and felt like I could no longer form words, language, or express myself in a way so as to be heard and seen. I felt like if I tried, then I would be misinterpreted and misunderstood.

Months later a friend sent me a card in the post, on it she wrote: "If you ever needed reminding that you are a good person, let this card be that reminder." I wept just as much then as I had done that evening in November. It was the reminder that I needed, a kind and thoughtful act of a friend that pulled me back from hopelessness. I don't know if she will ever know that she did that, but I should tell her. In fact, I will. It was this moment that began a process of deep self-reflection and I think marks the beginning of what I've recently come to see as some kind of recovery for me. Recovery is an interesting idea to get your head around, if you've never really thought of yourself as someone who needed to recover from anything. What I've realised is that I am recovering from myself.[4]

As bodies born into this world, we are blank and malleable. We are the direct product of a society that is not concerned with telling us to love who we are. Instead, we are presented with a series of fictitious ideals that makes us internalise a sense of inadequacy. This is true of people of colour, of women, of queer people, of the less-able-bodied; anyone who destabilises infrastructure, who threatens by their mere existence to destabilise order as defined by a white, capitalist, heteronormative, patriarchal centre ground. I think this is probably true of straight white men too, they just haven't realised it yet. Someone once described patriarchy as the "illness of the social body". Recovering ourselves from this illness, from this series of social practices, thought patterns and structures requires us to identify it before we extricate ourselves from it.

We are a generation and a culture woefully brought up on the idea of linear trajectories. They do not hold true. Progress is not linear. I think the realisation of this falsehood is something that many are struggling with right now. We are having to recalibrate, brought up on ideas and measures of success that, in the end, had no reward despite us doing everything that we were told to do in order to get there. We still seek those rewards, many of us, but the places where we might once have gone to look for them no longer deliver on that promise. In work, we crave deeper meaning. As bodies seeking physical and emotional connection, we fear we have become disposable. We are priced out of any notion of home ownership. Alongside this, we have absorbed messages from books and movies and magazines, most of which never catered to the reality of who we are, or cared for our experiences until it was profitable to do so.

4. Recovery is a word we hear a lot. Recovery suggests harking back to a past; a time or fixed state of being before something was lost. We may think of recovery as a process of regaining control of something stolen or adrift, of returning to some "normal" state of mind, health, and well-being. I like to think of it in terms of a recovery of the *self*, a rediscovery of my own sense of who I am. In this sense, I wonder perhaps if it is more helpful to think about this process as *discovery*.

I have struggled with bad sleep for two or more years now, often finding it impossible to fall asleep. I frequently lie in bed thinking about work, failed relationships, broken-down friendships. I think about having direction, having no direction. I think about having no real goals or understanding of why I'm doing what I'm doing. I think about how hard I find it to express myself sometimes. I think about rigged systems and racial injustices. I think about the hypocrisy and arrogance of political leaders. I think about our alarming lack of leaders. I think about having lived a life feeling constantly backed into silence. I think about how disillusionment has become a profession amongst me and my peers. I think about how some of the best minds of my generation are being tasked with selling trainers and detergent. I think about the everyday concessions and apologies we have to make as marginalised people; I think about how fucked it is that we are socialised to not even realise that we are doing it to ourselves. I think about the audacity of entitled white men. I think about the white men I've lambasted in the past and I think about how they had clearly never been told "no". I think about the misplaced air of self-importance of a younger generation that expresses itself online, tasked with the privilege of self-actualisation. I play out imaginary scenarios and fictions in my head, conversations and interactions between friends and colleagues that either took place or perhaps never took place. Sometimes I reimagine them with alternate endings. I think about things I wish I had said, fantasise about things I will say, regret the things I want to say but will never be brave enough to. These are just some of the things that keep me awake at night.

I remember the time after the EU referendum and the 2016 US election being an overwhelming period of news. It was at this point that I retreated into books, as this was the only place that I felt I could find quiet, calm, and honesty in and amongst the sheer wall of noise of public opinion and political punditry.[5] As we transitioned into the post-truth era and facts became fictions, it is no exaggeration to say that books saved my life. In these past months and years since, I have consumed and consumed as I seek to discover. I have immersed myself and found the most sense largely in the work of writers of colour, queer writers, mixed-race writers of colour, queer mixed-race writers of colour, the writing of

5. I wrote on an Instagram post: *Don't read the news. Read books instead. It's the only place you'll find 1. solace and 2. sense. To my shame it has taken me this long to get around to reading some Baldwin, but how true so many of his measured observations still hold today. As long as books keep getting published I reckon we'll be OK.*

women, of women of colour, feminist literature and feminist theory. Writers who occupy the margins but use their critical distance from power as power.[6]

It is, of course, hard to remain certain in a world where it feels like the rules are constantly being rewritten. Perhaps the trick is now to let go of all of these old expectations and to seize fresh opportunities. To regain control of the imagination. We are faced with an opportunity to redefine what our lives need to mean for us, and for us alone. We are existing through times where there are no reliable or encouraging models of reference before us when it comes to how to be, where there's a shortage of blueprints for being. The frameworks that do exist are no longer fit for purpose. Within all of this, perhaps we are presented with the opportunity for a renewed discovery of the self. To see ourselves clearly for the first time. It is through this discovery that I hope to find some new sense and understanding of what it means to be a body in this world.

So much of who I am and what I am doing remains unresolved. I have hit a particularly difficult and low point; the lowest I think I have probably ever hit. But I try to remind myself that this does not mean that the work I've done prior to this point has been a failure. When we create space for ourselves, we regain control of our own pace. I have come to value this idea of pace so much in the past few months. This is about finding my own way of speaking. In many ways, it's about learning to speak for the first time. So much of our time is spent using images to curate a perception of how successful and happy our lives are. I just wanted to spend some time using words to explain how awful I'm feeling. And I feel good about it. In doing so, I like to think I'm actually being kind to our language and perhaps more importantly, to myself. I am speaking to you from the margins and it is from here that I must write.

6. The assault on our identities begins from the moment we are born. We live in a culture that is obsessed with pointing the finger, that demands that people qualify who they are whilst offering no room to breathe. I am setting the pace and giving myself the space and time to discover who I am.

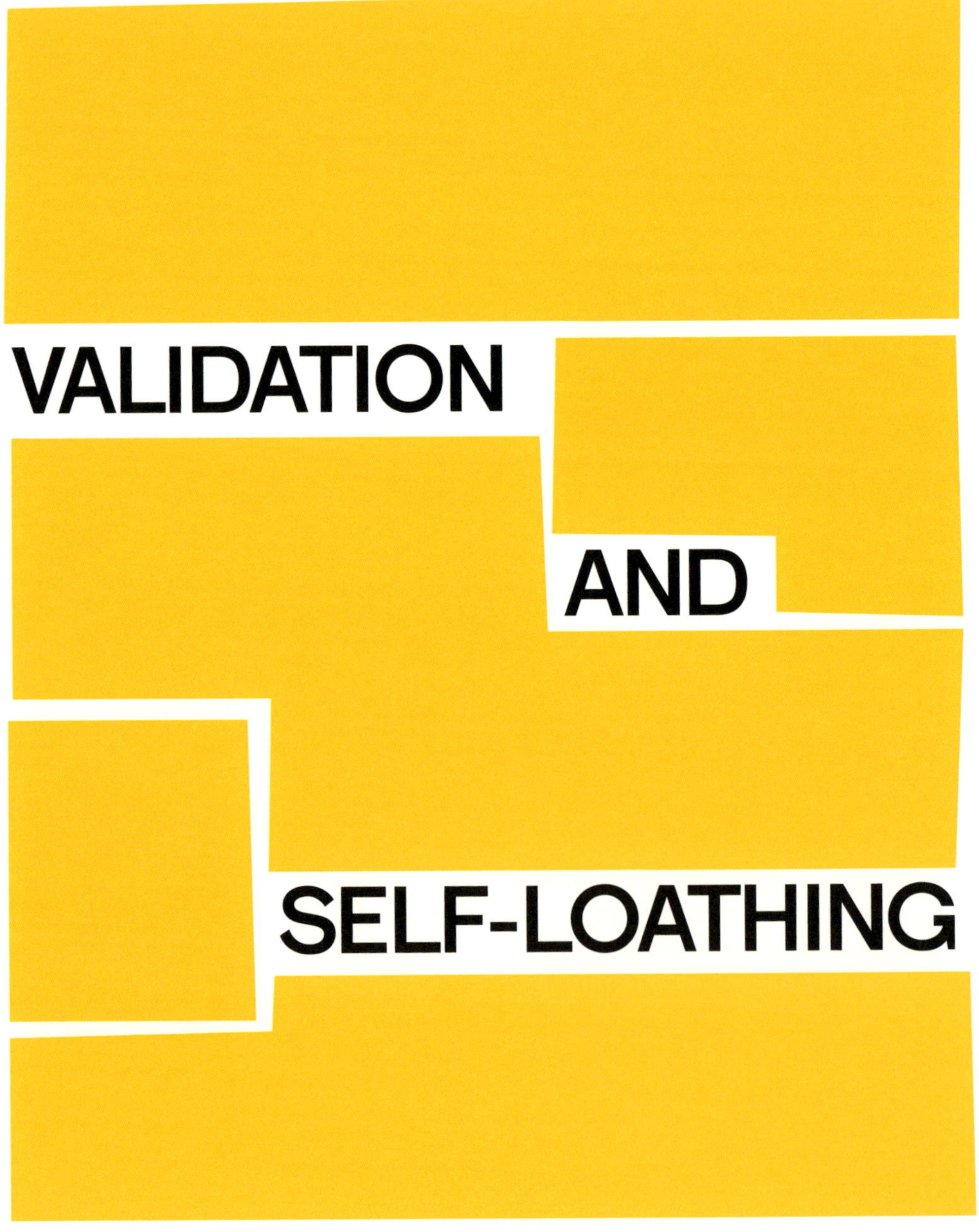
VALIDATION
AND
SELF-LOATHING

Words by Sam Judge

When my wife and I decided to get married, the stress of feeling like we needed to please so many people drove us to throw in the towel and elope to Vegas. Before we decided to go with a non-traditional ceremony, I'd made one decision synonymous with a modern western wedding: choosing a best man.

The man in question is my closest friend. We've been friends since the early 2000s when were both in the midst of puberty. He was then sporting an unruly mono-brow and a tight beaded necklace. I was afflicted with a voice that couldn't decide which register it wanted to be in and a pair of jeans made from enough material to clothe an entire family.

For a few years the only interest we shared was skateboarding. An avid punk fan, I never could get on board with his affinity for minimal house. However, not too long ago, I managed to summon enough stamina to convince him to power through his tiredness as we waited for an early morning set from Stephan Bodzin in Berlin's House of Weekend. Despite our lack of mutual interests we remain close. It could be laziness to find other friends but I'm sure it's more than that. I've no doubt it has a lot to do with our shared experiences with anxiety. They have, at times, been painfully similar. We have a level of understanding and empathy for each other's issues that is rare to find and has no doubt pulled me through desperate hours.

When I set out to make this magazine I knew I wanted his story to be in it. As I re-watch our recorded Skype call and begin the laborious process of transcription, I find myself smiling at how perfectly the weather outside matches the content of our conversation. It's dark, gloomy, and fucking miserable. But when he and I talk about these matters, as dark and gloomy as it may be, we often come out the other end with positivity. It's not wallowing but working through the nuts and bolts of the messy mind. Together, we attempt to make sense of the nonsense.

Rain like this—heavy, oppressive rain—always reminds me of a brief encounter I had with him many years ago. I was stood waiting for a bus, clinging to the bus shelter in an attempt to stay dry. I spotted a familiar figure slowly approaching. He was dragging his feet, taking the rain as it came, completely giving himself to the elements. No hood, no umbrella, his hair, face, and clothes were sodden. It seemed he had no urgency to be anywhere; a desultory trudge where the only destination was to escape his own mind.

It wasn't until he got much closer that I recognised the figure to be my friend. On any other day he'd have stopped and we'd have hung out for hours. On this day, he didn't feel like stopping. I knew it was about her but I didn't know what I could do. He trudged on, it seemed he couldn't get any wetter so why worry about more rain? I watched him disappear around a corner and continued to wait for my bus, only now with a pang of guilt; did he want me to pry him open or did he genuinely want to be alone?

What I witnessed was his first major episode of mental illness but it would take me some years to truly understand what that meant. This particular episode was ignited by a relationship mired in deceit that had come to its inevitable conclusion. The result: a young and hopeless man, convinced that he would never be enough for anyone.

In the years that followed, panic attacks, depression, and anxiety became the norm. He revealed to me that on some days he would wake up convinced that his brain was broken, with a feeling of complete detachment from being and existing. "On my worst days, 95 per cent of me is living between my ears," he joked. "I feel separated from my body and absent from everyone around me."

Each breakdown thereafter was the result of feeling inadequate. He recalled to me that during his adolescent years—that time when girls and existence are entwined—he felt a constant struggle for validation. Validation that he was attractive enough, athletic enough, funny enough, man enough. Many teenage boys share these same concerns, but for it to manifest itself in debilitating panic attacks is not so common. For him, it was a reality he now struggled to control. A text message, sent to a love interest with a double tick and no reply, would be enough to render shortness of breath and a fast-beating heart.

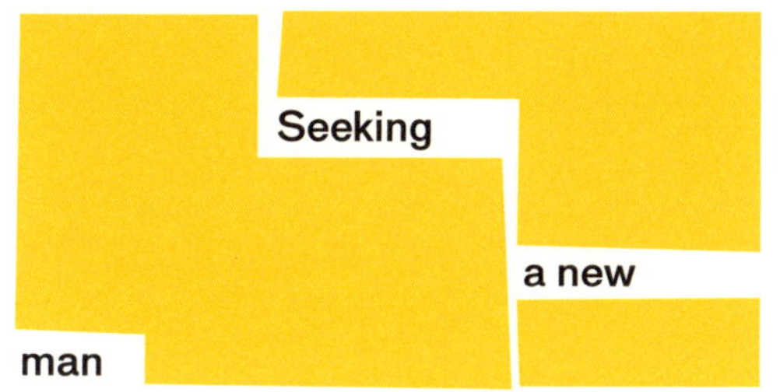

Seeking a new man

This obsession with inadequacy led him to pursue a life of self-improvement. He runs Tough Mudders, climbs for eight hours straight, and eats clean. When I asked why he goes to such lengths the answer seemed obvious, "When I live like that I know I'm always making steps to improve myself."

He extols the virtues of clean living not only for the physical benefits but the mental also. Despite this, there have been many periods where he has required medication and therapy to fight off the mental weather. "It feels like I've been on it all. Diazepam and Propranolol for the relentless onslaughts of panic attacks, and various strengths of Citalopram for general anxiety." He confessed that at one point he became engulfed in all the drugs. During a course of a heavy dose of Citalopram he committed an act of naïve rebellion and tossed them all in the bin. The result: he slept for a week solid, only to relapse two months later.

His experience with drugs mirrors his impressive résumé of talking therapies. Amongst our friends he's ribbed for being "tight"—he once returned his pint of water in a club after realising he would need to pay for it. Which makes it all the more shocking to hear that he estimates spending around £3,000 on private counselling over the years. Despite the cost of private therapies, he believes his most effective treatment was from NHS group cognitive behavioural therapy sessions. "It's quite simple," he reasoned. "CBT gave me the tools to deal with my issues myself."

He recalled the sobering experience of attending these classes. "In a room full of people with a myriad of mental health issues mine seemed smaller, easier, and less burdensome in comparison." He encountered people who struggled to leave the house and do basic tasks like food shopping, and people with skin-checking obsessions, believing that every mole would turn cancerous.

As he listed off these individual's struggles I found myself relating to some but also feeling thankful for not being afflicted with others. He recognised, though, that comparing mental health issues in this way is a futile exercise and that each person's struggle is their own and is relative to them. For him, his struggle can be best understood with the question, "Am I good enough to be everything for someone?" It's something he routinely asks himself. And yet, how ironic it is that I chose him to be *best man*. If only the validation of his friends were enough, he might feel a little less broken, a little more present, and a little more accepting of himself.

Contributors

A publication by Sam Judge Studio made possible by the following contributors:

Writer, Artist, Designer, Editor
Sam Judge
Instagram: @samjudgestudio

Photography
Michael Tom Walker
Instagram: @35mmmike

Contributing Writer
Will Oshiro de Groot
Twitter: @willdegroot

Contributing Editor
Kevin Braddock
Instagram: @torchlightsystem

Copy Editor
Grace Glendinning
Twitter: @thejoyoflooking

Press
Frazer Lawton
Enquiries: frazer@ryko.co

Get help

These helplines are available for those in need:

CALM Zone
0800 58 58 58

Samaritans
116 123

About Sam Judge

Sam Judge is a man. Born in Dudley in 1988, Sam attended art college multiple times and failed to graduate. He moved to London in 2009 to begin working as a designer. He has worked with some of the world's most well-known brands, including arts institutions, The Royal Academy of Arts and V&A.

Through his studio he explores personal and collaborative projects across a range of disciplines. *Disquiet: The Hidden Depths of Men* is one such project and his first self-published title. He hopes the project will be a valuable addition to the canon of publications on the topic of masculinity and will help continue to break the stigma surrounding mental illness in men.

First edition · October 2019

Printed in the UK by Pureprint and typeset in Maria by Phil Baber and Untitled Sans by Klim Type Foundry.

Independent Publishing Network
ISBN: 978-1-78972-588-9

samjudge.com